PRAYING IN THE
CELTIC SPIRIT

FRANCES M. KELLY

First published in 1999 by
KEVIN MAYHEW LTD
Buxhall
Stowmarket
Suffolk IP14 3BW

Compilation and notes © 1999 Frances M. Kelly

ISBN 1 84003 372 X
Catalogue No 1500272

Front cover
Hands of an Apostle (1508)
brush drawing by Albrecht Dürer (1471-1528)
Graphische Sammlung Albertina, Vienna
Bridgeman Art Library, London/New York
Background
Poppies by Alan Bedding

Cover design by Angela Palfrey
Series editor: Robert B. Kelly
Typesetting by Richard Weaver
Printed and bound in Great Britain

INTRODUCTION

This collection of prayers has been drawn mainly from the West Highlands of Scotland and from Ireland, although the traditional territories of the Celtic peoples also stretched down the Western coast of Britain through Wales to Brittany in France.

The tradition of the Celtic people is above all an oral one, transmitted in poetry, story-telling and song. Its expression in written form is always secondary and second-best – writing formalises, and destroys the personal warmth that oral transmission always has. Alexander Carmichael (1832-1912), who travelled the Western Isles and Highlands for 60 years collecting samples of this oral tradition, recounts how one old man shared a going-to-sleep rune with him. The next day the old man came back (which meant a 26-mile round trip) to make Carmichael promise his little prayer would not be published: 'Proud, indeed, shall I be if it give pleasure to yourself, but I should not like cold eyes to read it in a book' (*Carmina Gadelica* IV, p xxxi).

These prayers are necessarily those of particular individuals, shaped by their earthy experience and their rich imagination, but offering us in their own words what others passed on to them.

The Celtic Church inculturated parts of the clan and the druidic system: for example, the monastery, with the Abbot and the ordained monks supplanting the druidic brotherhood. The clan system, the extended family, also coloured the expression of the Celtic Church. This double sense of family may be the reason for the most striking feature of Celtic prayer: the affectionate, familiar way in which the Celts presume to speak to God.

God the Father is the Chief of chiefs, but like their clan chiefs, not a distant figurehead, rather a real, providing father-figure. Christ is addressed with a brotherly closeness. The power of the Spirit is confidently invoked. The place of the Trinity in these prayers is constant, very often in threefold invocations and blessings, which acknowledge the attributes of 'the Three' as filtered by the Celtic culture.

Before ever they were Christians, the Celts had a very vivid sense of the sacred, which permeated every aspect of their lives. To discover that God was the Creator of all things confirmed this spiritual instinct: nothing was beneath God's notice, no situation, no matter how mundane, was devoid of God. Through the eyes of faith, God was found in daily life, which thereby became a spontaneous liturgy of praise and supplication: even bathing the baby became a simple God-filled ritual, with a blessing for every handful of water poured.

Very little specifically Celtic survives of the Celtic Church of Patrick and Columba. Many of their manuscripts were lost to raids by Vikings, attracted by the gold and precious stones with which the Celts honoured their sacred books. Books, art and crosses were also destroyed in the fanatical frenzy of the Reformation. Meantime, the specifically Celtic rites had gradually died out.

However, the liturgy as celebrated today is firmly marked by the Celts. The Paschal fire which opens the Paschal Vigil is inherited from them. The feast of All Saints is a Christianisation of the Celtic New Year. The individual form of the sacrament of Penance – built on the traditional Celtic understanding of atonement and dependent on the abundance of monastic priests as spiritual guides – was one of the Celtic Church's inspired developments of the Church's tradition.

Formal traces of the Celtic Church may be few, but the great advantage of an oral tradition is that it has no need of documents, no need of official liturgies. A child hearing his parents praying would quite naturally pick up and continue the tradition. It is difficult to believe that centuries separate Saint Patrick and the prayers from Alexander Carmichael's *Carmina Gadelica* collection, so close are they in colour, concern and style.

What can we learn for our personal prayer today? Simply to recite these prayers would be to do them a great injustice. I cannot help thinking of Jesus' answer to the apostles when they asked him for a prayer; instead he taught them how to pray. This collection gives a flavour of how, around a profound sense of the presence of God, the Celtic peoples wove a personal pattern of blessing and petition, praise and invocation. We need to nurture our sense of the spiritual, retrain our eyes to see the world with a faith-vision, and in saying what we see, we shall be praying. Perhaps the hills, the lochs, the machairs, the wild or silvery-sanded beaches, the ever-present force of the ocean waves, are more conducive to such a faith-vision . . . But we all have friends, family who set out on journeys; babies to be bathed; we all lie down to sleep – human experiences which, when prayed, act as so many sacraments . . .

Frances M. Kelly

THE TRINITY

There can be few who have never heard of
Saint Patrick using a shamrock in preaching
on the Trinity. As always, there is a kernel of
truth behind the simple if colourful legend:
Saint Patrick was an inspired preacher on the
Trinity, who knew how to exploit the existing
culture and traditions of the Irish to help them
grasp this central mystery.

When Patrick came to Connaught, King Leogh-
ain's daughters demanded to know who was
this God Patrick preached, and where did he
live. Patrick replied:
'Our God is the God of all,
God of heaven and earth,
    sea and river.
He has dwelling in heaven and earth
    and sea and all that they contain.
He inspires all things;
he gives life to all living things.
It is he who kindles
    the light of the sun and the moon.
He has a Son,
    co-eternal with himself
    and like himself.
And the Holy Spirit breathes in them.
Father, Son and Holy Spirit,

are One and Undivided.
You are the daughters of a king of earth;
how I long to unite you
to the Son of Heaven!'

*In the great hymn attributed to Saint Patrick –
but which is probably a later composition –
the central theme is the power of the mystery
of the Trinity. But not as some abstract,
theological treatise: it is a poetic proclamation
of the personal indwelling of God, in the light
of which everything else is interpreted. Sometimes known as* The Cry of the Deer*, its more
traditional title is* The Lorica (Breastplate) of
Saint Patrick.

* The alternative title comes from the legend that, when
pursued by the Druids and pagan kings whose power he
threatened, Patrick and his monks seemed to take on the
shape of deer and so were able to escape them. This, the
legend says, is when Patrick sang this song: hence 'The
Cry of the Deer'.

THE LORICA OF SAINT PATRICK

I arise today
through a mighty strength,
the invocation of the Trinity,
through belief in the Threeness,
through confession of the Oneness
of the Creator of creation.

I arise today
   through the strength of Christ
      with his baptism,
   through the strength of his crucifixion
      with his burial
   through the strength of his resurrection
      with his ascension,
   through the strength of his descent
      for the judgment of doom.

I arise today
   through the strength of the love of
      Cherubim
   in obedience of angels,
   in the service of the archangels,
   in hope of resurrection
      to meet with reward,
   in the prayers of patriarchs,
   in predictions of prophets,
   in preaching of apostles,
   in faiths of confessors,
   in innocence of holy virgins,
   in deeds of righteous men.

I arise today,
   through the strength of heaven;
   light of sun, brilliance of moon,
   splendour of fire, speed of lightning,
   swiftness of wind, depth of sea,
   stability of earth, firmness of rock.

I arise today,
> through God's strength to pilot me:
> God's might to uphold me,
> God's wisdom to guide me,
> God's eye to look before me,
> God's ear to hear me,
> God's word to speak for me,
> God's hand to guard me,
> God's way to lie before me,
> God's shield to protect me,
> God's host to secure me:
>> from snares of devils,
>> from temptations of vices,
>> from inclinations of nature,
>> from everyone who shall wish me ill,
>>> afar and anear, alone and in a crowd.

I summon today
> all these powers between me and those evils:
>> against every cruel and merciless power
>>> that may oppose my body and my soul,
>> against incantations of false prophets,
>> against black laws of pagandom,
>> against false laws of heretics,
>> against craft of idolatry,
>> against spells of women
>>> and smiths and wizards,
>> against every knowledge
>>> that corrupts man's body and soul.

Christ to shield me today
 against poisoning,
 against burning,
 against drowning,
 against wounding,
 so that there may come to me
 abundance of reward.

Christ with me,
Christ before me,
Christ behind me,
Christ in me,
Christ beneath me,
Christ above me,
Christ on my right,
Christ on my left,
Christ in breadth,
Christ in length,
Christ when I lie down,
Christ when I sit down,
Christ when I arise,
Christ in the heart
 of every one who thinks of me,
Christ in the mouth
 of every one who speaks of me,
Christ in every eye
 that sees me,
Christ in every ear
 that hears me.

I arise today
  through a mighty strength,
  the invocation of the Trinity,
  through belief in the Threeness,
  through confession of the Oneness
    of the Creator of creation.

Salvation is of the Lord.
Salvation is of the Lord.
Salvation is of Christ.
May Thy Salvation, O Lord,
  be ever with us.

Attributed to Saint Patrick (c. 385-c. 461)
translation by Kuno Meyer (1858-1919) in
***Selections from Ancient Irish Poetry** (1911)*

The spiritual folklore of the Celtic peoples is full of triple incantations. Perhaps these threefold prayers, often accompanied by rites, echo some ancient pre-Christian practices (see the Birth-Baptism prayers, pp 44ff). At any rate, the mystery of the Trinity seems to have found natural expression among the Celts, for it completely permeates their threefold invocations and blessings.

Why such a natural affection for the Triune God? For a people whose life was founded on a firm sense of community and inter-dependence (the clan system), the Trinity certainly posed no theological problem. The Trinity was instinctively accepted as a 'family' group, where each is an individual, unique yet interdependent.

Examples of Trinitarian expressions can be found in practically all the sections that follow throughout the book.

TRIUNE OF GRACE

As it was, as it is,
    as it shall be evermore,
        O Triune of grace!
With the ebb, with the flow
    O Triune of grace!

Carmina Gadelica *II, 217*

TRINITY GRACE

The grace of God be with you,
    the grace of Christ be with you
    the grace of the Spirit be with you
        and with your children,
            for an hour, for ever, for eternity.

Carmina Gadelica *III, 21*

TRINITY BLESSING

God's blessing be yours,
   and well may it befall you;
Christ's blessing be yours,
   and well be you entreated;
Spirit's blessing be yours,
   and well spend you your lives,
      each day that you rise up,
      each night that you lie down.

***Carmina Gadelica** III, 211*

THE THREE

The Three who are over me,
   the Three who are below me,
   the Three who are above me here,
   the Three who are above me yonder;
   the Three who are in the earth,
   the Three who are in the air,
   the Three who are in the heaven,
   the Three who are in the great pouring sea.

***Carmina Gadelica** III, 93*

CHRIST

While deeply Trinitarian, Celtic spirituality was firmly Christ-centred. Christ is above all the Redeemer and Saviour, who has made us sons and daughters of God and won for us the right to enter the kingdom of Heaven.

The Celtic broad vision of the plan of salvation means that Christ's birth is understood and celebrated as a step toward the greater Paschal feast. Nor is it Easter as a past event, but as the Paschal mystery in which we are involved. We find in Celtic spirituality a firm echo of the Fathers of the Church: God draws near to us that we might draw near to God.

CHILD OF GLORY

The child of glory, the child of Mary,
   born in the stable, the King of all.
Who came to the wilderness and in our stead
   suffered;
    happy they are counted who to him are near.

When he himself saw that we were in travail
   heaven opened graciously over our head.
We beheld Christ, the Spirit of truth,
   the same drew us in 'neath the shield of
     his crown.

Strengthen our hope, enliven our joyance,
    keep us valiant, faithful and near,
O light of our lantern along with the virgins,
    singing in glory the anthem anew.

Carmina Gadelica III, 117

JESUS! JESUS! JESUS!

It were as easy for Jesus
    to renew the withered tree
    as to wither the new
    were it his will so to do.
        Jesus! Jesus! Jesus!
        Jesus! meet it were to praise him.

There is no plant in the ground
    but is full of his virtue,
    there is no form in the strand
    but is full of his blessing.
        Jesus! Jesus! Jesus!
        Jesus! meet it were to praise him.

There is no life in the sea,
    there is no creature in the river,
    there is naught in the firmament,
    but proclaims his goodness.
        Jesus! Jesus! Jesus!
        Jesus! meet it were to praise him.

There is no bird on the wing,
    there is no star in the sky,

there is nothing beneath the sun,
but proclaims his goodness.
    Jesus! Jesus! Jesus!
    Jesus! meet it were to praise him.

Carmina Gadelica *I, 39*

CHRIST, MY ENCIRCLER

Jesus! Only-begotten Son
    and Lamb of God the Father,
you gave your body's wine-blood
    to buy me from the grave-death.

    My Christ!
    My shield!
    My encircler!

    Each day, each night,
    each light, each dark.
    Be near me, uphold me,
    my treasure, my triumph.

In my lying, in my standing,
    in my watching, in my sleeping.

Jesus, Son of Mary!
    my helper, my encircler,
Jesus, Son of David,
    my strength everlasting;

Carmina Gadelica *III, 77*

His Feet Have Reached the Earth

This night is the eve of the great Nativity,
   born is the Son of Mary the Virgin,
   the soles of his feet have reached the earth,
   the Son of glory down from on high,
   heaven and earth glowed to him,
     All hail! let there be joy!

The peace of earth to him,
   the joy of heaven to him,
   behold his feet have reached the world;
   the homage of a King be his,
     the welcome of a Lamb be his.
King all victorious, Lamb all glorious,
   earth and ocean illumed to him,
     All hail! let there be joy!

The mountains glowed to him,
   the plains glowed to him,
   the voice of the waves
   with the song of the strand,
   announcing to us that Christ is born,
     Son of the King of kings
     from the land of salvation;
shone the sun on the mountains high to him,
     All hail! let there be joy!

Shone to him the earth and sphere together,
   God the Lord has opened a Door;
   Son of Mary Virgin, hasten to help me,

thou Christ of hope, thou Door of joy,
Golden Sun of hill and mountain,
 All hail! let there be joy!
   Carmina Gadelica I, 133

JOINT-HEIRS WITH CHRIST

Without any doubt,
 we shall rise on that day,
 in the clear light of the sun,
 that is, in the glory
 of Christ Jesus our Redeemer,
 as sons and daughters of the living God,
 and joint-heirs with Christ,
 conformed to his image,
 since of him and through him and with him
 we shall reign.
 . . .
We who believe in the true sun,
 that is, in Christ,
 and who do his will
 will never perish,
 but we will live for ever
 just as Christ lives for ever,
 reigning with God the Father almighty
 and the Holy Spirit,
 before all time, now
 and into all eternity. Amen.
   Confessions of Saint Patrick

MARY AND CHRIST

Mary the Dawn
   and Christ the Light of Day.
Mary the Gate
   and Christ the heav'nly Way.
Mary the Root
   and Christ the mystic Vine.
Mary the Grape
   and Christ the sacred Wine.
Mary the Beacon,
   Christ the haven's Rest.
Mary the Mirror,
   Christ the Vision Blest.

Unknown, quoted by John MacQuarrie
*in **Mary for all Christians***
(HarperCollins, 1990)

MARY AND THE BRANCH OF GLORY

O God,
   in my deeds,
   in my words,
   in my wishes,
   in my reason,
   and in the fulfilling of my desires
   may the blessed Virgin Mary
   and the promised Branch of Glory dwell.

In my sleep,
in my dreams,
in my repose
in my thoughts
in my heart and soul always
may the blessed Virgin Mary
and the promised Branch of Glory dwell.

Oh! in my heart and soul always
may the blessed Virgin Mary
and the fragrant Branch of Glory dwell.

Carmina Gadelica *I, 27*

ANGELS

A modern reader, used to a clear distinction between natural and supernatural, may be surprised by the space given to angels in Celtic prayer. In fact, a range of Gaelic expressions are translated simply as 'angel'. In the outer Hebrides they speak of 'comain', *which is simply* 'companion'.

Every time we celebrate the eucharist, we associate ourselves with the angels to sing the song from Isaiah's vision in the Temple, 'Holy, holy . . .'. For Celtic spirituality, where the whole world is the temple of God, the company and friendship of 'angels' is constant.

SHEPHERDING COMPANION

O angel of God who has charge of me
    from the dear Father of mercifulness,
    the shepherding kind of the fold of the saints
        to make round about me this night;

Drive from me every temptation and danger,
    surround me on the sea of unrighteousness,
    and in the narrows, crooks, and straits,
        keep my coracle, keep it always.

Be a bright flame before me,
    be a guiding star above me,

be a smooth path below me,
and be a kindly shepherd behind me,
   today, tonight, and for ever.

I am tired and I a stranger,
   lead me to the land of angels;
   for me it is time to go home
   to the court of Christ,
      to the peace of heaven.

Carmina Gadelica I, 49

PROTECTING COMPANION

God, give charge to your blessed angels
   to keep guard around this stead tonight,
   a band sacred, strong, and steadfast,
   that will shield this soul-shrine from harm.

Safeguard, O God, this household tonight,
   themselves and their means and their fame,
   deliver them from death, from distress, from harm,
   from the fruits of envy and of enmity.

Give to us, O God of peace,
   thankfulness despite our loss,
   to obey your statutes here below,
   and to enjoy yourself above.

Carmina Gadelica I, 91

MORNING, NOON AND NIGHT

Each morning began naturally with prayer and this set the tone for the rest of the day. Occasions for prayer throughout the day were endless since all things were seen to lead to God, or to have God hidden in them. They say that in the Celtic lands, the air between earth and heaven is 'thin' – even non-Celtic visitors to places like Iona sense this.

This sense of the sacred enhanced and transformed everyday tasks, taking them beyond the simply mundane. At the close of day God's presence was again called upon to protect, to encompass everyone and everything until the next day . . . or the next world, if God so willed.

AS THE MIST SCATTERS . . .

Thanks to you, O God,
   that I have risen today,
   to the rising of life itself.
May it be to your own glory,
   O God of every gift
   and to the glory of my soul likewise.

O great God,
   aid my soul
   with the aiding of your own mercy.
Even as I clothe my body with wool,

cover my soul
with the shadow of your wing.

Help me to avoid every sin,
and the source of every sin
to forsake.
And as the mist scatters on the crest of the hills
may each ill haze
clear from my soul, O God.

Carmina Gadelica *III, 31*

LOVE-GIFT

This day is your love-gift to me.
This dawn,
I take it from your hand.
Make me busy in your service
throughout its hours,
yet not so busy
that I cannot sing a happy song.
And may the south wind blow
its tenderness through my heart
so that I may bear myself gently towards all.
And may the sunshine of it
pass into my thoughts
so that each shall be
a picture of your thought,
noble and right.

Alistair MacLean in **Hebridean Altars**

KEEP ME

My soul's Healer,
   keep me at even,
   keep me at morning,
   keep me at noon.
On rough course faring,
   help and safeguard
   my means this night.
I am tired, astray, and stumbling,
   shield me
   from snare and sin.

Unknown

DEDICATION

Come I this day to the Father,
   come I this day to the Son,
   come I to the Holy Spirit powerful;
   come I this day with God,
   come I this day with Christ,
   come I with the Spirit of kindly balm.
God, and Spirit, and Jesus,
   from the crown of my head
   to the soles of my feet;
   come I with my reputation,
   come I with my testimony,
   come I to you, Jesus;
   Jesus, shelter me.

Unknown

TO SLEEP IN PEACE

I am now going into the sleep,
   be it that I in health shall waken;
   if death be to me in the death-sleep,
   be it that on your own arm,
   O God of Grace,
   I in peace shall waken.
Be it on your own beloved arm,
   O God of Grace,
   that I in peace shall waken.

Be my soul on your right hand, O God,
   you, King of the heaven of heavens;
   you it was who bought me with your blood,
   you it was who gave your life for me,
   encompass me this night, O God,
   that no harm, no evil shall me befall.

Whilst the body is dwelling in the sleep,
   the soul is soaring in the shadow of heaven,
   be the red-white Michael meeting the soul,
      early and late,
      night and day,
      early and late,
      night and day.
      Amen.

Carmina Gadelica *I, 85*

GUARD OUR SLEEP

May your holy angels,
  O Christ, son of living God,
  guard our sleep, our rest,
  our shining bed.

Let them reveal true visions
  to us in our sleep,
  O high-prince of the universe,
  O great king of the mysteries!

May no demons, no ill,
  no calamity or terrifying dreams
  disturb our rest,
  our willing, prompt repose.

May our watch be holy,
  our work, our task,
  our sleep, our rest
  without let, without break.

Attributed to Saint Patrick (c. 385-c. 461)
translation by Kuno Meyer (1858-1919)

YOU, O GREAT GOD

You, O great God,
  grant me your light,
  you, O great God,
  grant me your grace,

you, O great God,
   grant me your joy,
   and let me be made pure
   in the well of your health.

Lift from me, O God,
   my anguish.
Lift from me, O God,
   my abhorrence.
Lift from me, O God,
   all empty pride,
   and lighten my soul
   in the light of your love.

As I put off from me my raiment,
   grant me to put off my struggling;
   as the haze rises
      from off the crest of the mountains
   raise my soul from the vapour of death.

Jesus Christ, O Son of Mary,
Jesus Christ, O Paschal Son,
   shield my body
      in the shielding of your mantle
   and make pure my soul
      in the purifying of your grace.

Carmina Gadelica *III, 345*

FAMILY AND HOME

Family and kinship were the essence of community life, what gave it its sense of identity and marked life's contours. A web of interwoven prayers supported every life event.

How sad that in today's society, where the centrality of the family has been lost, such a web of prayer no longer seems natural. What a great gift to live in a community where everyone has a place: family, extended family, friends.

MY CHILDREN AND THINE

O thou,
   to whom
   to love and to be
   are one,
   hear my faith-cry
   for them who are
   more thine than mine.
Give each of them
   what is best for each.
I cannot tell what it is.
But thou knowest.
I can only ask that
   thou love them
   and keep them

with the loving and keeping
thou didst show
to Mary's Son and thine.

Alistair MacLean
in **Hebridean Altars**

BLESSING FOR A NEW HOME

Christ's cross upon your new home,
   Christ's cross upon your new hearth,
   Christ's cross upon your new dwelling,
   upon your newly-kindled fire.

Christ's cross upon your tallest grass,
   Christ's cross upon your fruitful partner
   Christ's cross upon your growing sons
   upon your growing daughters.

Christ's cross upon your household's helpers,
   Christ's cross upon the children yet unborn,
   Christ's cross upon the wise parents,
   upon your occupation.

Christ's cross upon your goods and income,
   Christ's cross upon your kith and kin,
   Christ's cross upon you in light or in darkness,
   each day and night of your lives.

Carmina Gadelica *III, 367*

BATHTIME BLESSING

A palmful for your age
  a palmful for your growth,
  a palmful for your throat,
  a flood for your appetite.

For your share of the dainty,
  crowdie and kail;
  for your share of the taking,
  honey and warm milk.

For your share of the supping,
  whisked whey and milk-product.

For your share of the spoil,
  with bow and with spear.

For your share of the preparation,
  the yellow eggs of Easter.

For your share of the treat,
  my treasure and my joy,

For your share of the feast
  with gifts and with tribute.

For your share of the treasure,
  pulset of my love.

For your share of the chase
  up the face of the Beinn-a-cheo.

For your share of the hunting
and the ruling over hosts.

For your share of palaces,
in the courts of kings.

For your share of Paradise
with its goodness and its peace.

The part of you that does not grow at dawn,
may it grow at eventide.

The part of you that does not grow at night,
may it grow at ridge of middle-day.

The three palmfuls
of the Secret Three,
to preserve you
from every envy,
evil eye and death;
the palmful of the God of Life,
the palmful of the Christ of Love,
the palmful of the Spirit of Peace,
Triune of Grace.

Carmina Gadelica I

crowdie = a kind of porridge
kail = cabbage
Beinn-a-cheo = the name of a mountain

YOUR CARE OUR PEACE

The Sacred Three
   my fortress be
   encircling me.
Come and be round
   my hearth,
   my home.

Fend you my kin
   and every sleeping thing within
   from scathe, from sin.
Your care our peace
   through mid of night,
   to night's release.

Alistair MacLean
*in **Hebridean Altars***

WEDDING BLESSING

May you know
   length of life
   and sun-filled days,
   and may you not have to depart this life
    before your own child
    falls in love.

Unknown (traditional Irish)

GOD'S PROTECTION

Bless, O God,
   the dwelling,
   and each who rests
   herein this night.

Bless, O God,
   my dear ones
   in every place
   wherein they sleep.

In the night that is tonight,
   and every single night;
   in the day that is today,
   and every single day.

Unknown

FIRE

In the cold Celtic lands fire was a practical necessity, providing warmth, heat for cooking, and light, too, on the dark winter nights. But beyond the practical, fire was symbolic.

Among pre-Christian Celts, a great sacred fire was lit in the spring, marking the end of winter. All fires, all lights were extinguished until the sacred fire was lit. Legend tells how Saint Patrick came to Tara where the King was to light the sacred pagan fire, collected wood and lit what for him was the Paschal fire. The druids warned the King that 'Unless this fire is extinguished immediately, its light will fill the whole of Ireland, and will burn until the end of time.'

The New Fire, which we light and bless as the opening ceremony of the Easter Vigil, is the Christianised successor of this ancient ritual, celebrating the victory of Light over darkness.

Even the ordinary household fire had a special meaning for the Celtic peoples. The ceremony of 'smooring' the fire at night would be performed symbolically and with loving care. The embers were spread evenly on the hearth in the middle of the floor, formed into a heaped circle and then divided into three sections around a boss in the centre. A peat was laid between each section with a prayer, so

36

*that the three peats were laid in the name of
Father, Son and Spirit; in the name of the God
of life, the God of peace and the God of grace.
The circle would then be covered with ashes
to dampen it down, so that it would burn
slowly during the night.*

*In the morning, before raising the peats so
that the fire would burst back into full life, the
woman prayed that the fire be blessed both to
the household it served and to the glory of
God who gave it.*

*Faith and the Christian life, like fire, need
careful attention if they are to stay alive . . .*

BLESSING OF THE SMOORING

I am smooring the fire
   as the Son of Mary would smoor;
   blest be the house, blest be the fire,
   blest be the people all.

Who are those down on the floor ?
John and Peter and Paul.
On whom is the vigil tonight ?
   on the fair gentle Mary and on her Son.

The mouth of God said,
   the angel of God spoke,
   an angel in the door of the house,
   to guard and to keep us all
   till comes daylight tomorrow.

Oh! may the angels of the Holy One of God
  environ me all this night.
Oh! may the angels of the Anointed One of God
  encompass me from harm and from evil,
  Oh! encompass me from harm this night.

Carmina Gadelica I

Smooring the Fire

The Sacred Three
  to save,
    to shield,
      to surround
  the hearth,
    the house,
      the household,
  this eve,
    this night.
Oh! this eve,
    this night,
      and every night,
        each single night. Amen.

Carmina Gadelica I, 235

Blessing of the Kindling

I will kindle my fire this morning
  in presence of the holy angels of heaven,
    without malice,
    without jealousy,
    without envy,
    without fear,
    without terror of any one under the sun,
  but the Holy Son of God to shield me.

God, kindle in my heart within
  a flame of love
    to my neighbour,
    to my foe,
    to my friend,
    to my kindred all,
    to the brave,
    to the knave,
    to the thrall,
  O Son of the loveliest Mary,
  from the lowliest thing that lives,
  to the Name that is highest of all.

***Carmina Gadelica** I, 231*

FOOD

From the ordinary to the festive, human food was clearly symbolic for the Celt. Here is a grace which moves effortlessly from body to soul; and a more colourful piece, which, even if the attribution to Bridget is suspect, shows the same simplicity of imagining heaven as the best of all possible feasts, beer included!

AT THE BREAKING OF BREAD

Be with me, O God,
    at the breaking of bread,
    be with me, O God,
    at the end of my meal;
    may no morsel
    of my body's partaking
    add to my soul's freight.

Carmina Gadelica *III*

BEER FOR THE KING OF KINGS

I would like to have
    the company of Heaven in my own house,
    with vats of good cheer laid out for them.
I would like to have
    the three Marys,
    their fame is so great.

I would like
    people from every corner of Heaven.
I would like
    them to be cheerful in their drinking.
I would like
    to have Jesus too, here among them.
I would like
    a great lake of beer for the King of kings.
I would like
    to be watching Heaven's family,
    drinking it through all eternity.

Attributed to St Bridget

HOSPITALITY

Ordinary human hospitality was and still is a hallmark of the Celtic peoples. But their Christian faith gives an added dimension to this cultural gift, for in this service of the visitor and the stranger, it is Christ who is welcomed. Not for nothing is Saint Martin of Tours frequently mentioned in Celtic texts, or carved onto Celtic crosses (for example, what must be Scotland's most magnificent Celtic cross, the early ninth century Saint Martin's Cross, still standing before the Abbey at Iona): he was the Roman soldier who shared his cloak with a beggar, only to discover later in a dream or vision that the beggar was Christ.

THE GUEST IS CHRIST

If there be a guest in your house
    and you conceal aught from him,
        'tis not the guest that will be without it,
    but Jesus, Mary's Son.

As translated by Kuno Meyer (1858-1919)
*in **Ancient Irish Poetry***

Rune of Hospitality

I saw a stranger yestreen,
  I put food in the eating place,
  drink in the drinking place,
  music in the listening place
  and in the sacred name of the Triune,
  he blessed myself and my house,
  my cattle and my dear ones.
And the lark said in her song
  'Often, often, often
  goes the Christ in the stranger's guise.'

From the **Book of Cerne** *(9th century)*
as translated in **A Pilgrim's Manual**
(Paulinus Press, 1985)

Hospitality Blessing

O King of stars!
  whether my house be dark or bright,
  never shall it be closed against any one,
  lest Christ close his house against me.

As translated by Kuno Meyer (1858-1919)
in **Ancient Irish Poetry**

BIRTH AND BAPTISM

A new-born baby was sometimes handed across the fire three times, then carried sunwise three times round the fire. In the name of the Trinity? In a reflection of some ancient pre-Christian rite?

In another triple ritual accompanied by a prayer in the name of the Trinity, the midwife would administer what was known as 'birth-baptism' (to distinguish it from the sacrament, which was called 'great baptism'). Here is how Alexander Carmichael (in his notes to Carmina Gadelica I) records what he was told by a midwife:

'When the image of the God of life is born into this world I put three little drops of water on the child's forehead. I put the first little drop in the name of the Father, and the watching-women say Amen. I put the second little drop in the name of the Son . . . the third little drop in the name of the Spirit.'

THE LITTLE DROP OF THE THREE

In name of God,
in name of Jesus,
in name of Spirit,
the perfect Three of power.

The little drop of the Father
  on your little forehead, beloved one.

The little drop of the Son
  on your little forehead, beloved one.

The little drop of the Spirit
  on your little forehead, beloved one.

To aid you, to guard you,
  to shield you, to surround you.

To keep you from the fays,
  to shield you from the host.

To sain you from the gnome,
  to deliver you from the spectre.

The little drop of water from the Three
  to shield you from sorrow.

The little drop of the Three
  to fill you with their pleasantness.

The little drop of the Three
  to fill you with their virtue.

Oh! the little drop of the Three
  to fill you with their virtue.

Carmina Gadelica III, 17

BIRTH-BAPTISM

In the name of Father,	Amen.
In the name of Son,	Amen.
In the name of Spirit,	Amen.
Three to lave thee,	Amen.
Three to bathe thee,	Amen.
Three to save thee,	Amen.
Father and Son and Spirit.	Amen.
Father and Son and Spirit.	Amen.
Father and Son and Spirit.	Amen.

Carmina Gadelica III, 11

A SMALL DROP OF WATER . . .

A small drop of water
   to your forehead, beloved,
   meet for Father, Son and Spirit,
   the Triune of power.

A small drop of water
   to encompass my beloved,
   meet for Father, Son and Spirit,
   the Triune of power.

A small drop of water
   to fill you with each grace,
   meet for Father, Son and Spirit,
   the Triune of power.

Carmina Gadelica III, 21

Sprinkle Your Grace . . .

Sprinkle down upon him
  your grace,
    give to him
      virtue and growth,
    give to him
      strength and guidance,
    give to him
      flocks and possessions,
sense and reason void of guile;
that he may stand without reproach
    in your presence.

Unknown

Nine Waves of Grace

A small wave for your form.
A small wave for your voice.
A small wave for your speech.
A small wave for your means.
A small wave for your generosity.
A small wave for your appetite.
A small wave for your wealth.
A small wave for your life.
A small wave for your health.

Nine waves of grace upon you,
    waves of the Giver of Health.

Carmina Gadelica III

DEATH

Celtic spirituality uses two great metaphors for death: journey and sleep.

For a people who were renowned travellers, death was the ultimate and greatest journey. Just as those setting out on an ordinary journey would be accompanied by blessing songs (see pp 53ff), so the family and friends would encircle the dead person, and led by 'a soul-friend' (anam chara) would sing the death blessing, known as 'soul-leading' or 'soul-peace'. Often this song imagined Christ, saints or angels coming out to meet and bring the dead one home.

In some of the prayers it is difficult to discern whether it is simply a night prayer (see prayers on pages 27-28), or a prayer concerning death, so interwoven are the two senses of sleep. It is almost as if ordinary sleep is a rehearsal for death, which is 'restoring sleep'.

RESTORING SLEEP

You are going home this night
   to your home of winter
   to your home of autumn,
   of spring, and of summer.
You are going home this night
   to your perpetual home

to your eternal bed
to your eternal slumber.

Sleep you, sleep,
    and away with your sorrow!
Sleep you, sleep,
    and away with your sorrow!
Sleep you, sleep,
    and away with your sorrow!
Sleep, my beloved,
    in the Rock of the fold.
Sleep this night
    in the breast of your Mother.
Sleep, my beloved,
    while she herself soothes you.
Sleep you this night
    on the Virgin's arm.
Sleep, my beloved,
    while she herself kisses you.

The great sleep of Jesus,
    the surpassing sleep of Jesus.
The sleep of Jesus' wound,
    the sleep of Jesus' grief.
The young sleep of Jesus,
    the restoring sleep of Jesus.
The sleep of the kiss of Jesus
    of peace and glory.
The sleep of the seven lights
    be yours, beloved.

The sleep of the seven joys
  be yours, beloved.
The sleep of the seven slumbers
  be yours, beloved.
On the arm of the Jesus of blessings,
  the Christ of grace.

The shade of death
  lies upon your face, beloved,
  but the Jesus of grace
    has his hand about you;
  in nearness to the Trinity
    farewell to your pains,
  Christ stands before you
    and peace is in his mind.

Sleep, O sleep
  in the calm of all calm.
Sleep, O sleep
  in the guidance of guidance.
Sleep, O sleep
  in the love of all loves.
Sleep, O sleep
  in the Lord of life!
Sleep, O beloved
  in the God of life!

Carmina Gadelica III, 383-385

MY LIFE'S JOURNEY

As you were
   before
      at my life's beginning,
so be you
   again
      at my journey's end.

As you were
   beside me
      at my soul's shaping,
Father, be there
   too,
      at my journey's close.

Carmina Gadelica III, 66

SMOOTHING THE WAY

Be each saint in heaven,
   each sainted woman in heaven,
   each angel in heaven
   stretching their arms for you
   smoothing the way for you
   when you go thither
      over the river hard to see.

Oh! when you go thither home
   over the river hard to see.

Carmina Gadelica III, 203

SOUL PEACE

Since you, O Christ, it was
  who did buy the soul –
    at the time of yielding the life,
    at the time of pouring the sweat,
    at the time of offering the clay,
    at the time of shedding the blood,
    at the time of balancing the beam,
    at the time of severing the breath,
    at the time of delivering the judgment,
    be its peace upon your own ingathering.

Jesus Christ, Son of gentle Mary,
  be its peace upon your own ingathering,
    O Jesus! upon your own ingathering.

And may Michael white kindly,
  high king of the holy angels,
  take possession of the beloved soul,
  and shield it home
          to the Three of surpassing love,
  Oh! to the Three of surpassing love.

***Carmina Gadelica** I, 121*

JOURNEYING

*The Celtic peoples were legendary travellers.
For the Celtic monks, this was considered part
of their vocation – 'like Abraham', Columba
told his community.*

*There seems to be a sense in the various
prayers that one never really journeys alone,
but always in the presence of God, a presence
expressed explicitly in blessings. Some of
the prayers are said by the traveller. However,
if someone was setting out on a long or a par-
ticularly dangerous journey, family and friends
would gather to send the traveller on their way
with a prayer. Some would then walk with the
traveller for the early part of the journey,
singing the blessing together.*

BLESSING FOR THE TRAVELLER

May God make safe to you
   each steep,
may God make safe to you
   each pass,
may God make safe to you
   each road
and may he take you in the clasp
   of his own two hands.
Carmina Gadelica *III, 203*

RUNE OF THE ROAD

May the road rise with you.
May the wind be always at your back.
May the sun shine warm upon your face,
   the rain fall soft upon your fields.
And until we meet again
   may God hold you in the palm of his hand.

Carmina Gadelica *IV*

WITH THE PROTECTION OF CHRIST

I set the keeping of Christ about you,
   I set the guarding of God with you,
   to possess you, to protect you
      from drowning,
   from danger,
   from loss.

The Gospel of the God of grace
   be from your summit to your sole;
   the Gospel of Christ, King of salvation,
      be as a mantle
      to your body.

Nor drownèd be you at sea,
   nor slain be you on land,
   nor o'erborne be you by man
      nor undone be you
      by woman!

Carmina Gadelica *III, 193*

BLESS MY JOURNEY

Bless to me, O God,
   the earth beneath my foot.
Bless to me, O God,
   the path whereon I go.

Bless to me, O God,
   the thing of my desire.
Thou evermore of evermore,
   Bless thou to me my rest.

Bless to me the things
   whereon is set my mind.
Bless to me the things
   whereon is set my love.

Bless to me the things
   whereon is set my hope;
O thou King of kings,
   bless thou to me mine eye!

Carmina Gadelica *III, 181*

EACH STEP OF YOUR JOURNEY

God be with you on every hill,
   Spirit be with you on every stream,
   headland and ridge and lawn;
   each sea, each land,
   each moor and meadow;
   each lying down,
   each rising up;
   in the trough of the waves,
   on the crest of the billows;
   each step of your journey.

   Carmina Gadelica *III, 195*

FISHERMAN'S PRAYER

Lord, the sea is large,
   and my boat is so small.

From Brittany

PERSONAL PRAYERS
OF PETITION

Personal prayers speak for themselves, in a way – but it is worth noting the sense of dedication to the ideals of the Gospel. Christ is called on and we are called upon to be and to bring Christ to others.

EACH DAY, EACH NIGHT

May I speak each day according to your justice,
    each day may I show your chastening, O God;
    may I speak each day according
        to your wisdom,
    each day and night may I be at peace
        with you.

Each day may I count the causes of your mercy,
    may I each day give heed to your laws;
    each day may I compose to you a song,
    may I harp each day your praise, O God.

May I each day give love to you, Jesus,
    each night may I do the same;
    each day and night, dark and light,
    may I praise your goodness to me, O God.

***Carmina Gadelica** I, 51*

GOD, CHRIST AND ME

God's will would I do,
   my own will bridle;
God's due would I give,
   my own due yield;
God's path would I travel,
   my own path refuse.

Christ's death would I ponder,
   my own death remember;
Christ's agony would I meditate,
   my love to God make warmer;
Christ's cross would I carry,
   my own cross forget.

Repentance of sin would I make,
   early repentance choose;
   a bridle to my tongue I would put,
   a bridle on my thoughts I would keep.

God's judgment would I judge,
   my own judgment guard;
Christ's redemption would I seize,
   my own ransom work;
the love of Christ would I feel,
   my own love know.

Unknown

I Wish . . .

Many a time I wish
   I were other than I am.
I am weary of the solemn tide;
   of the little fields,
   of this brooding isle.

I long to be rid
   of the weight of duty
   and to have my part
   in ampler life.

O you, who are wisdom and pity both,
   set me free
     from the lordship of desire.

Help me to find my happiness
   in my acceptance
     of what is my purpose:
   in friendly eyes;
   in work well done;
   in quietness born of trust;
   and – most of all –
   in the awareness
     of your presence in my spirit.

Alistair MacLean
in **Hebridean Altars**

MY PRAYER

'Tis from my mouth
   that my prayer I say,
'tis from my heart
     that my prayer I pray,
'tis before you
     that my prayer I lay.

To yourself, O healing hand,
  I call,
  O you, Son of God,
  who heals us all.

from G. R. D. Mclean's
Poems of the Western Highlanders

BLESSING PRAYERS
FOR OTHERS

What greater gift could be given than that of a prayer? A belief in the value and power of prayer made prayer something worth offering to others. If someone was going on a long journey a prayer was often written on a piece of parchment and sewn into the clothing as a blessing for the traveller, a reminder of those who would always be with them in prayer.

GLADNESS AND PLENTY

Each day be glad to you,
　　no day be sad to you,
　　life rich and satisfying.

Plenty be on your course,
　　a son be on your coming,
　　a daughter on your arriving.

The strong help of the servant be yours,
　　the strong help of the fire be yours,
　　the strong help of the graces.

The love-death of joy be yours,
　　the love-death of Mary be yours,
　　the loving arm of your Saviour.

Carmina Gadelica *III, 235*

A LIFE BLESSING

I pray for you a joyous life,
    honour, estate and a good repute,
    no sigh from your heart
    no tear from your eye.

No hindrance on your path,
    no shadow on your face,
    until you lie down in that mansion
    in the arms of Christ benign.

Carmina Gadelica *III, 239*

FURTHER READING

Pride of place, for serious scholars of Celtic spirituality, must go to the magnificent collection by Alexander Carmichael, which runs to six volumes:

Carmina Gadelica, Scottish Academic Press, Edinburgh.

Volume I of *Carmina Gadelica* can be consulted on internet, in both the original Gaelic and in Alexander Carmichael's English translation:

www.smo.ahi.ac.uk/gaidhlig/corpus/Carmina/

Carmina Gadelica covers traditional folklore from the highlands and islands of Scotland, some of which is clearly pagan, and some of which is a curious blend of pagan and Christian. For those who prefer to remain within the Christian Celtic spiritual tradition, there are various anthologies (i.e. selections from *Carmina Gadelica*) by Esther de Waal:

God Under My Roof. Celtic songs and blessings (SLG Press, Oxford, 1984)

Threshold of Light: prayers and praises from the Celtic tradition (Darton, Longman & Todd, London)

The Celtic Vision. Selections from Carmina Gadelica (Darton, Longman & Todd, London, 1988)

For prolonged meditation on classic Celtic sources, and an example of how personal prayer today can be inspired by these sources, there are the two books by David Adam:

The Edge of Glory: prayers in the Celtic tradition (Triangle/SPCK, 1985)

The Cry of the Deer. Meditations on the hymn of Saint Patrick (Triangle/SPCK, 1987)

Other sources of interest (in chronological order):

The Poem-Book of the Gael, edited by Eleanor Hull (Chatto & Windus, 1912)

Selections from Ancient Irish Poetry translated by Kuno Meyer (Constable, 1911)

Ancient Irish Poetry, translated by Kuno Meyer (Constable, 1913)

Hebridean Altars by Alistair MacLean (Moray Press, 1937)